100 Important Life Lessons For Everyone

100 Important Life Lessons For Everyone

Practical Lessons to Help You Achieve a Happy & Successful Life
VOLUME 1

Gina Johnson Smith

iUniverse, Inc.
New York Lincoln Shanghai

100 Important Life Lessons for Everyone
Practical Lessons to Help You Achieve a Happy & Successful Life
VOLUME 1

iUniverse, Inc.

For information address:
iUniverse
2021 Pine Lake Road, Suite 100
Lincoln, NE 68512
www.iuniverse.com

Unless Indicated, all bible scripture taken from the New King James Version

ISBN: 0-595-28290-3

Printed in the United States of America

Dedication

This book is dedicated to all the children in my life.

Always be willing to gain wisdom, examine your inner self, and skillfully apply that which you have learned to your own life. When you do this, God will always honor His word.

To Brandon LaShawn Mumford, my angelic grandson who now resides with the Lord. Your sweet life was brief, but more purposeful than most. Because of you, my life and the lives of many were profoundly touched and magnificently transformed. What a tremendous blessing you proved to be.

The wisdom of your experiences is a gift you can share.

It is like this: When I was a child, I spoke and thought and reasoned as a child does. But when I became a man my thoughts grew far beyond those of my childhood and now I have put away the childish things. In the same way, we can see and understand only a little about God now; as if we were peering at his reflection in a poor mirror; but someday we are going to see him in his completeness, face to face. Now all that I know is hazy and blurred, but then I will see everything clearly, just as clearly as God sees into my heart right now.

1 Corinthians 13:11-12 Living Bible Translation

Contents

ME, MYSELF & I

MY SPIRITUAL SELF

THE PARENT IN ME

MISCELLANEOUS

CAREER

Acknowledgements

First, I want to thank my Lord and Savior Jesus Christ. For without You Lord, there would be no me. All praises and glory to you!

To my dear departed grandmother, Lillie Roberta Williams, my mother Marcella Goodwin, and my dad, Arthur Johnson. The winds beneath my wings. *Bigmama*, you were the light of my life and you still live in my heart!

My husband Rube, one of the best and most consistent examples of a Godly man I have ever had in my life. You are my teacher, my mentor, and the love of my life. You have helped me become the woman God intended me to be.

I could not have completed this book without the guidance and support of some wonderful people: Pastor, Dr. Elder Garon Harden, Sr. and First Lady Elect Sister Harden of Greater Open Door Church of God in Christ, for their ministering to my life and that of my family. I am truly blessed to include these individuals as my spiritual guides.

I also want to acknowledge the continued support and friendship of Nadine Brown, publisher and editor of the Walnut Times Magazine and Pastor Tommy and Dr. Gloria Morrow, publishers of the Inland Valley News, as well as Mr. Richard Love, publisher of the Long Beach Times. Thank you all for your belief in my writing ability and providing me a forum to "have my say". I love and respect you all.

A big thank you also goes out to Deborah Smith Pegues, first a friend, and then a sister-in-law, who continued to rally me with this project, and who's prayers over this project and over my life have sustained me. Thank you Deborah.

Additional thanks to my sister and friend, Ellen Arlon, for being my sounding board and providing sisterly encouragement and constructive criticism. My good friend and fellow writer Sonya Mohammed, for never letting the long lapses in our fellowship impact our great friendship.

To my co-workers at SYSCO Food Services of Los Angeles, and the President and CEO, Bruce J. Schwartz. Bruce has been my friend and family, and has for years been one of the best examples of how a parent, boss, leader, and human being should be. I salute you and the rest of our SYSCO family. You all have been my rock during the past few years of challenges. A very special thanks to

Tom Jones and Peter Quelch for showing support and interest in my talent and helping to keep my dream alive. You will never know the extent of my gratitude.

And finally, a loving thank you to my husband Rube, our sons Chris and Demel, our daughters Enjoli and Shawnda, and our grandchildren, Chanel, Kailon, and DJ, for giving me support, unconditional love, and the space and understanding I needed to research, write, rewrite, talk to myself, rewrite, cry and finally, turn out a publishable book. I dearly love you all.

Introduction

This book began as a journal, listing lessons from my life. After getting the hits and knocks that come with wrong choices, I finally woke up, took stock, and began to evaluate my actions and their consequences. After taking off the blinders that hid my life only from me, I began to see the toll my actions had taken on my life and the lives of those around me. In this exposure of my whole life to me, I learned to look realistically at what I was doing to cause my life to be the way I didn't want it to be. Soon after I began the long, slow process of making the necessary changes in my life. This journey began the labor pains that ultimately gave birth to this book.

These life lessons are not ones you can learn in school. Some of the most important of life's lessons cannot be taught in school. Instead our precious God extracts these lessons from our everyday steps and experiences. And be assured the lessons He sends always applies. Most of these lessons are ones that others have shared with me or I have come to learn through the school of hard knocks. The goal of *100 Life Lessons for Everyone* is to wake us up from inaction, fear and lack of wisdom and knowledge. It is a call to renew our minds. And in that renewal, take the necessary action to improve the quality of our *whole* lives. It is designed to be a book that's simple and straightforward. This project has become a passion of mine. Why do I have a burning desire to reach you? Because I've been you. I've done stuff and learned lessons. And through my learning, through my lessons, I hope to spare other's from learning these lessons the hard way.

While not all of life's lessons are listed here, some tremendously important one's are. Some of these lessons will remind you of your own experiences, others will truly make you think. But most importantly, this book will give you the tools you need to evaluate yourself, begin the process of making the necessary changes, and get through this life being successful in your spirit, mind, and body.

I am a survivor. And I believe a survivor's job is to retell her story for the generations to come. While you may not agree with everything said, I challenge you to keep an open mind and most importantly, an open heart. Good reading!

ME, MYSELF & I

1 BE HONEST WITH YOURSELF ABOUT YOURSELF

It's time to get real with yourself about your life and everybody in it. Be truthful about what isn't working in your life. Stop making excuses and start making results. Keep in mind, how others treat you is a result of what you have allowed over the course of the relationship. How you are treated is in direct proportion to the boundaries you have or have not set in the relationship.

We have to be true to those important areas in our lives. Acknowledge the unvarnished, unadulterated truth about yourself to yourself. Stop lying to yourself. What are you or aren't you doing that is destructive to your life? Are you uncomfortable with others overstepping your boundaries but you wont say anything to them? Do you blow up with others after repeated offenses instead of confronting the offense head on in a loving way? If so, you aren't being honest with them about your boundaries. It's not their fault—they have no boundary line to stop them. Establish boundaries, and communicate that boundary in a loving way to others, and expect them to honor it. Along with this you have to also have consequences for not honoring your boundary. Most of the people in your life want your fellowship. If your boundaries have the consequence of lack of fellowship, you can bet eventually they will honor it. Maybe not at first, but eventually they will.

Are you honest about your strengths and weaknesses to yourself? Get to really know yourself. Learn what your weaknesses are. Accepting your role in your problems means that you understand that the solution lies within you. If you have a weakness in a certain area, get educated. Don't get defensive and put down those that have done the work. Don't make excuses for yourself. Just do what you have to do to improve things for yourself. If your credit rating is terrible, don't make it everyone else's fault or *"the system"*, take responsibility for your part and take the necessary steps to improve it. TODAY. I define responsibility as the ability to respond to life. "Response—able". You have the ability to choose how to respond to life. Decide today to end all the excuses, lies and conning yourself about what's going on. There is a Chinese Proverb that says, "teachers can open the door, but you must enter by yourself." Remember, the beginning of growth is when you begin to personally accept responsibility for your choices.

2 DON'T GET MAD, GET MOTIVATED

I have always found the best way to get even with someone that gossips about you or tries to hurt you or your reputation is not to get mad, but to get motivated to do what you need to do to define your life. My daughter went through a very rough period several years ago. She was rebellious, thought she had all the answers, dealt with all the wrong people, and paid a price. In the last few years she has grown into a responsible person. Despite this growth, others didn't naturally believe she had had a change of heart. She was hurt and wasted a lot of time being mad at others. I helped her to see that expending energy getting mad is a waste of time. Over the course of these few years she had to learn that those that viewed her, as a rebel would not immediately accept her "reformed" ways. They would have to see over time that this was a real transformation. In the meantime she would need to understand that she had established how everyone would view her by her past behavior. The amount of time it took her to destroy the good perception people had of her, would be equal or greater to the time it would take re-establishing it. In the meantime, she was to do all she could to get her life back on track. She discovered she needed the hurt to motivate her to action. She learned that pain is a greater motivator than pleasure. She moved ahead swiftly, has made the honor roll at her school over and over, and has organized her life to the point that she is on top of her game, level headed, and her life is headed in the right direction. Sometime we have to get indicted to get motivated to move forward.

What about when we are treated wrong because of racism or sexism of just because of jealousness or pettiness on someone else's part? You will find there are many things in life that you can do nothing to change—like people who will prejudge you. If you allow them to upset you, then you lose. Let it go. Learn to ignore and desensitize yourself to these attacks. Don't let the opinions of others dictate who you are. The only opinion of you that matter's is the one you have of yourself. Take time today to overcome the negative thrown at you by others and allow it to motivate you to greatness!

3 DON'T EXPEND ENERGY LOOKING BACK—MOVE FORWARD

All of us have some form of negative "stuff" in our past. Things we aren't proud of. Things we wish we had done differently. We cannot take the past back. Events of long ago have permanently altered all that we are and purposely change us into whom we become. The past is over and the future hasn't happened yet. The "lessons" of our past were for a reason, and if we have learned our lessons and have grown beyond the lesson, we shouldn't keep revisiting them. We must remember the lessons of the past, but not live in the pain of it. Revisiting the pain of the past is neither healthy nor helpful. Yesterday is a cancelled check; tomorrow is a promissory note; today is the only cash you have, so spend it wisely. You can't move forward looking back. Decide today not to give your power away with anger, jealousy, laziness, worry or bitterness.

4 LEARN TO LIVE WITH WHAT YOU CANNOT CHANGE

God grant me the serenity to change the things that I can change, accept the things that I can't, and the wisdom to know the difference (paraphrased). Our lives are made up of people and things we don't' necessarily agree with. While there are some things we can change, there are others we simply can't. When you can't change a thing or a situation, adjust your attitude and approach. When you do this, you allow yourself the ability to work around that which you cannot change. We cannot direct the wind, but we can adjust the sails.

Most of us have not been dealt a great hand in life. Our lives are not easy. We don't have the big house, the perfect car, or even the best relationships. You must learn to play the hand you are dealt. It takes very little skill to play a good hand, but exceptional skill to play a poor hand. Learn to turn your disadvantages into advantages by seeing possibilities where others see problems.

5 DON'T TAKE A FALSE SENSE OF RESPONSIBILITY

Do you have adult children that refuse to take responsibility for their lives? How about siblings that can never seem to keep a job or a roof over they're own head? We've all been here before. The difference between those that have and get out of that "support" mentality and those that seem to stay on that treadmill is the ability to release responsibility.

You are not the General Manager of the universe. A very wise friend of mine once said that we are to provide support without removing responsibility. By that, it is meant that you should provide opportunities for that person to pull himself or herself up, and then only if they are ready to do the work to move forward. If they're not ready, all the money and help in the world won't work. Don't allow others to make you their God by over dependence on you and don't let the expectations of others manipulate you. Even God doesn't try to please everyone and only a fool would try to do what God won't do.

While we should help others we should not take responsibility for their lives—they should! Extend yourself with help only as far as you are comfortable, which should be just before you begin complaining to others about how much you have to do! Because once you begin complaining, you've overstepped your boundaries. We are responsible TO people, not FOR them.

6 TAKE CARE OF YOURSELF

This applies to two situations. First, take care of yourself in the sense that your life is your responsibility. Not anyone else's. If you get into debt it is your responsibility to get out. It is not everyone else's place to rescue you over and over. Look at your life seriously. Understand that there are consequences for the decisions that you make. Don't let your desire to have a $400 pair of boots today get you into financial trouble tomorrow. While others can and will help you, counting on that help could be disastrous. Remember, you are account-able for your own life. Good or bad, successful or not, happy or sad, fair or unfair, you own your life.

Secondly, take care of yourself in the sense that you are responsible for your health. Our best requires rest. Don't expect that others will back off and give you a break. They won't. When you need a break, you have to take one. Don't worry about everyone else feeling neglected, this is about your health. If you don't take care of your own health, no one else will. If you don't take time off, your body will make time off. We are not designed to go without rest. It is important to regularly rest your body, recharge your emotions, and refocus your spirit.

7 DON'T HAVE A VICTIM MENTALITY

Do you generally feel that people are talking about you? If you are ethnic do you believe that is the root of your problem? If you answer yes to either of these, its time you stopped having a victim mentality, stop being offended. Yes, maybe they are talking about you, maybe life does seem unfair, but dwelling on how victimized you are will never change anything. By convincing yourself that you are a victim, you are guaranteed to have no progress, no healing, and no victory. When you run away from the responsibility for your life, you deny yourself the opportunity to take the reins in your own hands to control your own life. Something to think about: You may complain about the way people react to you, but whether you realize it or not you may be helping create their reaction through your actions. Take a moment to evaluate yourself. Bottom line: *get over it.* Most people won't change; you can only change your reaction to them.

I have learned that people that don't know you (and some that do) will fault find, gossip about you, and be catty and a whole assortment of reactions for their own selfish, self-serving reasons. It is their problem. Don't make it yours. Know who you are. Value yourself and do your best at whatever you do. That's all that's important. And if you really get down to it, if you are a child of God, you shouldn't in any way believe that your color or circumstances makes a difference in anything. For us, race shouldn't be an issue. God overrules race. God can make anything happen that he wants to happen, anytime, any place, in any situation. We are supposed to exist in a different place than the rest world.

If you are serious about your life, don't give others that kind of power over your life.

8 THE ONLY PERSON YOU CAN CHANGE IS YOU

Most people are fixers. We like to fix people into how we think they should be. Then we get frustrated when they don't get it, when they don't see our "vision". The most liberating feeling in the world is realizing that you can only change you—not other people. People change based on their realization that they need to change, and their desire to do so. Until they reach that point, all the hopin' and a prayin', the wishin' and pressurin' won't mean a thing. Have you ever noticed when you don't expend energy trying to control or change other people, you feel good? Be selective about where you will spend your energy. By all means help others change when they desire to do so, but use your own energy to improve yourself. The person you spend the most time with is you. The person you most need the power to influence and control is you.

9 WHAT YOU CHOOSE TO SURROUND YOURSELF WITH YOU BECOME

You've heard the statement "garbage in, garbage out". Your mind is more powerful than a computer. You allow messages in your mind from teachers, friends, parents, television, radio, movies, etc. Your internal program determines your perceptions, self-esteem and ultimately your behavior.

If you want to change your internal program, remember you are the programmer. You will need to install wisdom and knowledge and delete some habits and relationships. Self-examination and self-correction are the hot keys. What you choose to surround yourself with becomes a part of who you are. Have you ever notice that as you grow in life, in experiences, in education, the circle of people you call your friends changes? Our friends are a result of what we are most comfortable with—what areas in our life we spend the most time in.

If you surround yourself with individuals with no goals, no ambition, you will eventually become like those individuals. Likewise, if your surround yourself with serious minded individuals, you will take on that demeanor. It is your choice.

10 BE PATIENT WITH OTHERS—THEY ARE NOT YOU

Most of us catch on quickly. We move fast and expect others to do likewise. Patience is defined as capable of calmly awaiting an outcome, not impulsive. Most often we get aggravated with others when they don't grasp concepts as quickly as we do or perform tasks like we do, or even think like we do! I have learned that we are all on a learning journey. And on this journey, some of us are further down the line than others. Some of us may never get as far as others. But all of us are learning what is necessary for our own individual lives and purposes.

Be willing to listen to take the time to listen to other's explanations. Don't just jump ahead, assuming that you know why they did a certain thing, only to find out after the explanation that you were wrong. Yes, patience is a virtue, and it's a virtue worth striving for.

11 YOUR APPEARANCE SPEAKS VOLUMES

Recently my husband and I had a conversation with our eldest son about the value of appearance. He is working and moving up into a corporate environment. While he does and outstanding job at what he does, his appearance screams *"teen-ager. Not ready for prime time! Problem maker, keep on alert!"* He blew us off by saying he does a great job and his manager knows it and will back him up. Good luck!

Several studies I have read state that people make a judgment of you within the first 5 minutes of meeting you. They take in your physical appearance, what you say, and with that they render judgment on you. While it isn't fair, it is a reality. One of the most important choices we make daily is how we present and define ourselves to others. When you are in a situation that determines whether you get an opportunity, play all your cards. Don't' let appearances be your downfall.

Our son told us that he was going to be "true to himself". We applauded his decision, but reminded him that sometimes if "true to yourself" costs you the opportunity to earn money to be self sufficient, he might want to rethink that position. Now, that is not to say that he should sell himself down the river for money, or overstep a core value for money. But let's be practical, we're talking about clothes here! Most 20-somethings will rarely win a job after interviewing with their pants hanging below the rear-end and earrings in the ear.

If compromise is not your thing, just remember, your choices have consequences for you—not for others supporting or helping you. If you want to honor your choices, accept the consequences without complaining. While the consequences may not be fair, that's the way it is.

12 MIND YOUR OWN BUSINESS

When we focus on accomplishing what we need to accomplish, we don't have time to worry about what others are doing with their lives.

It is a good rule to avoid all gossip. I like the scripture in Philippians 4:8 that states *"Whatever is true, what ever is noble, whatever is right, whatever is pure, whatever is lovely, whatever is admirable, if anything is excellent or praise worthy, to think about such things."* If your conversation is not encouraging another or if it is not of a "good report", it's probably best to avoid it.

Remember, how others choose to live their lives is *not your business*. While you may not agree with their choices, if you are not supporting them—paying their bills, putting a roof over their head—if they are self-supporting, functional adults, they have earned the right to live their lives as they see fit. Their life is between them and God. Not only do they have this right, they are also responsible for the consequences of their choices. That is the beauty of being an adult. If you love that person and see them behave in ways that will negatively impact their lives, by all means let them know. But remember, it is their choice to follow your advise or not. We are not judge, jury and executioner. Our job is to share truth, pray for them, encourage them, and love them anyway.

13 OPEN YOURSELF TO CHANGE

Change is an inevitable part of our lives. It is the only thing we can be certain of in life. Like the metamorphosis of a butterfly, we will transition from one state to another some time in our lives, because each change represents a move to our purpose.

Change is defined as "to make difference, to take an alternate course or direction, to undergo a process." One of the ways change happens is in expanding relationships. When you get married, it changes the dynamics of both families. Everyone in each family that is involved with those individuals has a responsibility to understand that the newly married person's life will change. That newly married person now has other responsibilities and priorities, and their priority to their new unit should be respected. That's why the Bible is clear on the statement regarding marriage that "*...for this cause shall a man leave father and mother, and shall cleave to his wife; and they two shall be one flesh...What therefore God hath joined together, let not man put asunder.*"(Matthew 19:5-6). This scripture supports that the new family should now be allowed to become one, and further supports that change is not only necessary for growth and bonding—or becoming one, but a requirement of God.

Change is also important in friendships. Throughout life we have friends that best support where we currently are in our lives. Sometimes one will grow in a different direction. One may get married while the other remains single. While the friendship is maintained, sometimes it is not possible to spend the same amount of time and energy on that relationship as you did previously. That married person now has different priorities. When this happens, we must remember not to get upset with our friends, not to discard them, but to understand that change is a part of life.

As you move into change, realize you are moving into territory that is not familiar and you probably aren't going to like it at first because most of us feel safe when we don't attempt to change and feel threatened when we do. Prepare yourself for the changes that are bound to take place in your life. Look ahead in your life. Mentally begin to prepare yourself for your children growing up. Look at what their needs will be in high school. A car? College? Prepare yourself for them leaving home, getting married. How will you treat your future in-laws? Begin the process of preparing yourself for getting older, for your spouse's death. Will you be able to live on your own? How will you survive?

Will you have the income to live on your own? Will you want to live by yourself? Will you have to live with your children? What about a nursing home?

Change? Stress? Risk? While it is frightening, great risk brought with it great reward for Ruth in the Old Testament. As a young woman she stepped out of her circle of security, crossed the hills to Bethlehem and took on a new country, new religion, new family, new everything. Making this dramatic change brought her into the lineage of King David. Without change, it would never have occurred.

There will always be a part of us that wants to hold on to tradition, to the safe, to the comfortable, to the way its always been. But like Ruth, we can trust that change—even unwanted change—can be the beginning of exciting growth.

Remember, change begins with you. It is not contingent upon another person making a change first. It is a solitary act of your own will. Take the time today to realize the inevitableness of change. There are seasons in life where change will be the rule of the day. Graciously adjust your attitude and move forward.

14 DON'T LET YOUR EMOTIONS RULE

Most of the problems we have in relationships have to do with letting our emotion rule. Too often we ruin opportunities by being offended. Offense kills more relationships and more opportunities that we will ever know.

The children's rhyme *"sticks and stones may break bone, my but words will never hurt me,"* is a complete lie. Words not only hurt, they kill our spirit. I have learned that when you don't know WHO you are and WHOSE you are, you will be offended by just about everything. Now, does it mean I never get offended? Of course it doesn't. But I have learned that I can recover quicker because I realize the importance of not letting my emotions get the best of me.

Move beyond offense to looking at why that person would choose to hurt you with words. Remember, hurting people hurt people. Try to look beyond what they are saying to hurt you to see where *they* are hurting. You just might bring someone back from the edge if you take the focus off yourself and put it on him or her.

Most women let their emotions rule. It's the way we are made. We make emotion-based decisions. In the Garden of Eden, Eve was provoked by emotion to make the decision to eat of the forbidden fruit. Then she brought Adam into the mix by emotionally leading him to eat, and you know the rest—everything went down from there. Whether making a decision about a relationship, a job choice, a friend, regarding money, it is important that we look at the pros and cons of our decisions. It's alright to experience your emotions, but don't live in them. Don't let your emotions rule.

15 SOME THINGS SHOULD GO WITH YOU TO THE GRAVE

Our lives have been a succession of the good and the bad things we have done. Most of us haven't done horrendous things, but we've done some things that will hurt others if revealed. If your revelation doesn't help heal someone else's hurt, it is better not to reveal it to anyone. When I say "*anyone*" that qualifies as your best friend, you neighbor, your lay counselor—anyone who could or would reveal it, use it against you or the other person. I always say it's best to take it with you to the grave. I am a firm believer in not destroying someone else's life just to clear my conscious. If it doesn't in some positive way help someone else, let it go. Most of us have enough disappointment in our lives. Don't add to it.

16 FIND YOUR PURPOSE
AND STAY FOCUSED

Our life is not a mere collection of days and months. We all have a purpose for our lives. We are here for a reason. When you find your purpose everything flows. Orison Sweet Marden said, *"A will finds a way"*. Everything works seamlessly when our purpose is revealed. I have found greatness to be present in all of us. We were all brought into this world with a mission. We have been given everything it takes to achieve our mission. We only have to tap into and develop the gifts and talents that God has blessed us with.

Everyone's purpose is not the same, but everyone's purpose has to do with encouraging or helping others journey to truth. As you focus on your goals and the purpose for your life, you will be surprised at the people you will attract to assist you in bringing that mission to life.

Discovery of your purpose will bring fulfillment to your life. How do you find your purpose? Look at those things in your life that seem to come easy to you. Look for the clues in the things you love to do. It's there in you. Others may not recognize it. That's okay. We all have it within us. Decide today that you will welcome opportunity to serve and love others. Incorporate your gifts with areas that support the growth and encouragement of others, and you will be on your way.

17 ENLARGE YOUR WORLD

Enlarging your world has to do with expanding your environment. Introducing your life to other experiences, your taste buds to other flavors. If you have spent your whole life in the area where you grew up, never left, never experienced the other side of town, another state, another country, it is time to do it. If you stick to the familiar steak and eggs, its time to experience a different dish.

When we stay locked in our familiar, safe world, we cheat ourselves out of experiencing and growing in ways we would never have realized. Does that mean abandon your familiar? No. But every person will benefit from seeing things from another perspective.

When my children were growing up it was important to me that they be exposed to the ballet, listening to classical music, hip-hop, jazz, and country music—the whole gamut. Of course they didn't like some of the music, but they found they enjoyed the calming effect of classical, they learned to appreciate jazz. The result has been that they have become well-rounded people.

Take the time to enlarge your world. It is not selling out. Some things you will find acceptable, others you will reject. It is your choice. When you enlarge your world, you expand your possibilities.

18 BE SUPPORTIVE OF THE ELDERLY

My dad and mother-in-law are currently in their later years. Both have experienced many changes that hinder their ability to operate as they once did. What is it like to still have the same thoughts, the same feelings; enfolded in flesh that fails you? Seeing yourself deteriorate rapidly, watching that time clock tick-tock, running out. Not to mention the gradual deterioration of the mind, the lost or locked memories.

These are some of the things our aged feel daily. With these feelings comes frustration. With frustration sometimes come outbursts. This is a time for mutual support and respect. While living with them may not always work, providing a comfortable, stress free environment is important for they're well being.

Our aging parents have a responsibility as well. They have a responsibility not to take for granted the assistance and support their children provide. A good friend of mine is fond of saying that we become more like ourselves as we age. If this is true, we take on our true behavior. What does that say about us as we age? Keep in mind; age is never an excuse for rudeness or cruelty. Your children don't owe you their lives. They owe it to you to grow up and be decent, productive, God-fearing people. Remember, they are juggling a lot of responsibilities along with assisting you. Appreciation and cooperation on both ends will make things work smoother. While you may not feel as you should, *feelings* should never dictate how you treat others.

When both children and aged parents work together, our aged parents can best enjoy the golden years of their lives.

19 WATCH YOUR WORDS

"Your blessing or cursing is in your mouth." (Proverb 10:21). *"Death and life are in the power of the tongue, and those who love it will eat its fruit."* (Proverb 18:21) This is a spiritual law that few Christians have a grasp on. Yet, these scriptures are perhaps a few of the most powerful and awesome scriptures in the Bible. Its implication is staggering to our minds when we realize that God has put whether we succeed or fail in life into our own hands through the words of our mouth.

Our words have a tremendous amount of power. All that we are is the result of what we have thought and said. What you believe is determined by what you subconscious is exposed to by the environment, nutrition, conversations, past memories, books, news media, peers, family, and a host of other influences. Words, images, and feelings make lasting impressions on your mind like water on silk. If you don't like what you're experiencing in your life right now, you can positively change the results by changing your thoughts and words right now. Not only can our words hurt or heal our lives, our words have the ability to hurt or heal individuals. When we call our children *"stupid"* and a host of other negative names, we potentially harm them. Subconsciously we take in what we hear and it becomes a part of who we become. We have the power to make our life and the lives of those around us positive and potentially success-ful, or we can destroy those same lives. It is up to us.

20 MIND YOUR MANNERS

There was a time when manners were expected. At that time it was required of children to display their *"home training"*. These days most adults and children alike aren't sure what they should or shouldn't do since the rules aren't clearly defined. We need to make etiquette training a requirement.

Young people that display proper manners, will stand out, since it is no longer the norm. My children have found this to be true and it has helped open doors to them that would not necessarily open to youth their age.

Look at your own life. What are some areas you can brush up on? Writing thank you notes for gifts given, or hospitality shown at another's home. Something simple like returning things back to their original place and in its original condition is another way to display good manners.

Take the time to brush up on your etiquette. These days etiquette classes are available everywhere. This is one of the greatest investments you can make in your life and that of your children. The benefits will be profound.

21 BE YOUR OWN BEST FRIEND

While it is great to have close friends, sometimes you need to maintain your own base as your own best friend. Sometimes you need to be your own rooting section. Sometimes you need to motivate yourself. Others generally won't understand your goals, where you are reaching for and will unconsciously try to keep you in your *"safety zone"*. It is at times like that that you have to step out, trust the spirit in you, pray, and move forward.

In this life you will do your own living and your own dying. Most people will never completely see your vision like you do. What they cannot clearly see, they cannot clearly support. People hear and incorporate only what they understand. The Lord is the only one who will be there when husbands, jobs, and money are gone.

Learn how to be secure in your own solitude. The more patience and time you give to this area of growth, the less likely you are to become a needy person emotionally, sexually, or financially. Learn to drink the robust wine of your own life. Get to be your own best friend.

22 MAINTAIN YOUR OWN INTERESTS APART FROM YOUR MATE

We are all individuals. Even in relationships it is important to maintain your own identity and your own interests. That's what made you attractive in the first place. We each have our own individual missions to achieve with the gifts and talents we've been given. Don't allow your vision or mission to be incapacitated because you fear standing on your own. Cling to the truth that God is doing a good work in you. Each of us needs our own vision and our own walk with God. This does not knock unity with your mate, but too much of anything is not good. While we stand together, we must also stand on our own.

When we maintain our own interests, work towards our vision, we are able to bring something fresh and interesting to the relationship, while growing together into the people we are destined to be.

23 DON'T FORGET TO JUDGE YOURSELF WITH THE EQUAL WEIGHT THAT YOU JUDGE OTHERS

We need to work at not destroying other's for wrongdoing. We all have failed along the way. And along that way someone extended us grace and allowed us to move beyond our faults. Are you livid with others when they cut you off on the road, but find nothing really wrong with it when you do the same to others?

I have found when we focus the same amount of judgment on ourselves that we put on others; we tend back off others and are more understanding.

It is important to remember daily to look at our own selves before we condemn others.

24 ADMIT WHEN YOU'RE WRONG

Sometimes this is the hardest thing for us to learn. We make excuses, we blame others, and we do whatever we have to do to keep from admitting our wrongness. The beginning of change is to admit our wrongs or faults.

This is especially important when it comes to our children. When you are wrong and your children know you are wrong, and instead of admitting fault we get defensive and take the stance of "I'm the parent and don't question me". When we do this we lose our credibility with our children and in the process we are teaching them to lie their way out instead of facing the music for their choices.

We will never go to the next level of growth if we cannot honestly look at ourselves, admit any wrong doing, and begin the process of making change. Remember, the beginning of growth comes only when we are brave enough to look at our selves under the razor sharp light of truth, humble ourselves, and admit our wrongs.

25 RESPECT YOURSELF

Respecting oneself has to do with how we allow others to treat us and how we treat ourselves. Many of us women haven't learned to respect ourselves. We give up our physical affections in exchange for the love we think we'll get. What we end up with is being used and getting disrespected. From there our self-esteem takes a major dive.

When we respect ourselves we don't do things to hurt our lives. When we lack respect for ourselves, we make choices that are unhealthy for our lives. And these choices ultimately cause hurt and humiliation. This pain causes us to loose self-respect and ultimately our self-esteem. Respecting ourselves means waiting. It means honoring our bodies by abstaining. Abstinence doesn't just mean for women, but for men as well. We are all precious beings. Our love, our bodies, our hearts are special and shouldn't be wasted on a momentary thrill.

Respecting ourselves also means honoring our minds by not filling it with garbage music that scars our souls, but instead filling it with uplifting music and entertainment. We can't truly respect anyone else until we learn to respect and appreciate ourselves.

26 MAKE A DECISION AND TAKE ACTION

Life doesn't reward quitters. Through quitting you may reward yourself with a false peace, but it comes at the price of your dreams. Until knowledge and understanding is translated into action, they are of no value. This one step—choosing a goal and sticking to it—changes everything. Don't get stuck in indecision. A life decision is one that has been made from the heart. It is a conviction you live by all the time. The indispensable first step to getting the things you want out of life is to decide what you want, then taking the necessary action to have faith, use your gifts, and go after it.

If you've made up your mind that you can do something, you're absolutely right. On the flip side, if you believe you can't do it, you're absolutely right. Decide today to make a decision, take action, and work towards your goals—whatever they may be—performing the step by step actions that will get you there.

MY SPIRITUAL SELF

27 DO YOUR PART AND TRUST GOD FOR THE REST

Deut. 28:1-14

We often forget that the Lord doesn't work alone. We seem to forget that the Lord EXPECTS something from us. There are requirements for us. When we pray for God to increase us, we only get it when we qualify for it. First we have to do our best to be living the life we are required to live, secondly we have to ask for guidance, and thirdly we are to use the talents and gifts that we have been blessed with, then wait on Him for the rest. We don't have to convince others, connive, or cheat. We just have to trust that He will come through with what we ask for, in the way it is best for us, in His time.

Your gift is the key to the manifestation to your desires. The book of Timothy encourages us to *"stir up the gift that is in thee."* Develop your gifts (your part), trust the Lord to open the door to opportunity (your faith in His part), and move on the opportunities presented to you (His part in action). If your life is going to get better, it will be because you *make it better.* Pray to God, but row for the shore.

28 FAITH WITHOUT WORKS IS DEAD

James 2:18-26

Often I hear Christians say, *"just have faith"*. But really, what does that mean? Having faith is a part of the equation, but you have to DO something as well. You have to LIVE out the word, or at least in your heart be working towards doing right.

In James 2:18 the scripture says, *"Show me your faith without deeds and I will show you my faith by what I do."* A good example of this is when God told Abraham to bring Isaac as a sacrifice. Isaac was Abraham's beloved son. Because of Abraham's faith, he was obedient and brought Isaac. While preparing to offer Isaac for sacrifice, an angel descended and told him to not to touch the boy, but to look over in the bush and there would be a ram to use as a sacrifice. Abraham had unyielding faith in God. If God only gave him his son for a season, fine. If God would provide a sacrifice, fine. Whatever was the will of God, he would continue to be obedient.

Abraham brought Isaac (he did the action). We are required to take action. When you ask God for something, begin the process of preparing yourself. If you want a greater income, prepare yourself for it. Develop your gifts. When you are ready, God will open the doors to the opportunities that will bring into manifestation what you have asked.

29 WE ARE BLESSED TO BE A BLESSING

Acts 20:35 Deuteronomy 5:7-8

Many of us have good, if not great jobs. We are able to supply our life and the lives of those that we love with many extras that we ordinarily wouldn't be able to afford. We need to always remember that we have more than enough so we can help others. Does that mean that I am to respond to everyone's need? No. God is not moved by my emotion, and neither should we be. The spirit will lead you to help, when appropriate. I truly believe we get in the way of helping others learn to trust in God when we consistently meet their need. We become their source and they never get to see God act on their behalf for themselves. This can be very dangerous for you. Sometimes God wants a person to experience low times because generally when people are at their lowest—when they don't have an answer—that's when they seek God. That's when he has their attention. If we continue to provide for them, eventually God will block our ability to help them to keep us out of the way, and that block may impact my own life circumstances. The people in your life have to eventually learn that God is their source—not you.

When I am lead to give, I have learned not to worry about what others will do with what I give them—that's between them and God. God will reward me regardless of what they do. He just wants my obedience. Through blessing others, we open the door to our being blessed more (the principle of sowing and reaping), and through that, we help others to see the Lords goodness manifested in his people.

30 ONLY STEP OUT
AS FAR AS YOUR FAITH IS

Romans 12:3-

Many people believe faith equals risk. This is certainly true. Faith is defined as going to the edge with all we have and know and taking one more step. When we step out on faith, we are trusting that God will bring it—what we want—to pass. But there is a difference between faith and presumption. We are not to presume that we can put our family in jeopardy in the name of *"trusting in the Lord"*.

Everyone has been given a measure of faith, but everyone's faith is at a different place because of what we have seen manifested in our lives. I may be able to believe for a $1 million dollar home, while my friend may only be able to believe the Lord to cure her cold. That doesn't make her less *"spiritual"* than me, but it means that I have seen my faith manifested more consistently, and therefore can believe for more.

Faith is a growing thing. You grow in this area based on what you are seeing manifested. Keep working at it, so your faith will keep growing. When I say, step out only as far as your faith is, what I mean is don't forgo medication if you are critically ill when you run the gamut between faith and doubt, faith and unbelief, back to faith and unbelief. In this case your faith won't work and you'll find yourself in the hospital, or worse dead.

Take your time in the area of faith. Begin small with areas you can wait to see what you ask for manifested. You have to be willing to wait on God and endure any and all until He answers. Risk reasonably, risk responsibly, risk within the level of your faith.

31 CHOOSE TO BE JOYFUL

Psalms 30:5

Abe Lincoln said most people are about as happy as they make up their minds to be. Being joyful or happy is a choice. Sure, there will always be opportunities for unhappiness. Ecclesiastes 3:1 says *"To everything there is a season and a time and a purpose under the heaven"*. At those midnight hours you can experience your sorrow, but an attitude of gratefulness is always the order of the day.

Joyfulness has nothing to do with your circumstances—what you have, or how you life. Joyfulness has to do with an inner peace. This peace is only obtained through the realization that you have a savior, and no matter what the circumstances, if you endure to the end, you will be victorious. That is the peace that passes understanding. I have learned that we choose our attitude. It doesn't have to be reflective of circumstances or feelings.

When things are at their most difficult, focus on your blessings. In respect to our blessings you'll find your problems are small. When we keep this perspective, it lessens our need to fault find or be unhappy. Keep this in mind when the desire to be unhappy creeps in.

32 GOD IS SOVEREIGN. HE DOESN'T HAVE TO CONSULT US

Job 38:3-18, 40:1-2

This has to be the most profound lesson I have learned. Several years ago I lost my grandson at two months old. This loss was tremendously devastating to my family and I. I was so grief stricken. We couldn't understand why God allowed this to happen.

Later many of my co-workers questioned why a good God would allow this to happen. I shared with them what I was forced to understand. God is sovereign. He sees the big picture and makes his decisions based on it, not necessarily what I want. Like a parent, he knows ultimately what's best and whether I realize it or not, He has my best interests at heart.

God's sovereignty is played out beautifully in the story of Job. Job was a perfect and upright man in the sight of God. He was blessed with great wealth. Satan believed that Job would curse God to His face if he removed the hedge of protection from Job's life. In a test, God allowed Satan to move on Jobs' possessions, family, and ultimately his physical person. While Job got discouraged, he did not curse God. In the end because of Job's faithfulness, God restored all that Job had and more. Like Job, if we truly believe that God loves us, we will defer to His decisions and not defect from Him.

As parents, we sometimes have to make unpopular decisions. We have to make hard choices. We have to do this because we see a larger picture than our children. And while they kick and scream, say they hate us, we still must do what we have to do. God is no different. As our King, he is not influenced by our wishes. He is in charge. He sees a larger picture. He has a bigger plan. And yes, He does love us.

33 IT'S ABOUT RELATIONSHIP

Deuteronomy 6:5

I attend a wonderful church. But many of the activities of the church are simply that—activities for fellowship. They have nothing to do with your relationship with Christ. Too often we join church like we join women's clubs. Church becomes our social gathering, and oftentimes the root of the activities has nothing to do with learning more about Christ, worship or anything. Church becomes a social club. Be very careful about this.

Don't be a religious Christian. Attending church is about encountering Christ. It is about learning more of what it is to live out the word—or be more like Jesus. Learn to reach through the veil of church and find Christ.

It's great if you attend a church that promotes a lot of activities. But remember your primary responsibility is to study and grow in the word. Fellowship with your congregation is important for accountability, but fellowship with Christ is the key.

34 GET SERIOUS ABOUT YOUR SPIRITUAL WALK

➡

Psalms 55:19

Have you completed committed your life to Christ? Or are you holding on to the world in some areas. I'll go to church, but I'll cheat on my wife on Saturday night? I'll stop cursing, but I'll steal extra supplies from my job. While these may not be your situations, you know in your heart if you are straddling the fence. It's time to get on one side or the other. In Revelations 3:15-16, the word is clear about Gods feelings about lack of commitment. *"I know thy works, that thou art neither cold nor hot. I would thou went cold or hot. So then because thou art lukewarm and neither cold nor hot, I will spew thee out of my mouth."* Also Psalms 55:19, *"God shall hear, and afflict them even he who abideth of old. Selah. Because they do not change, therefore they fear not God."* These are very strong statements about believers who decide not to walk in what they have learned. There is great responsibility in application of what you have learned. We are accountable for what we know to do. When we don't do what we *know* to do, we risk greater consequences.

We have to make a decision to begin the process of moving in one direction—God's direction. We can't keep making one step forward and three steps backwards. This is counter-productive and will keep our lives cursed. You will develop your wisdom teeth when you read your bible and make a decision to put into practice what you have learned.

Begin today to make a commitment to let go of ways that curse your life. Choose today whom you will serve.

35 HE DIDN'T PROMISE YOU
A ROSE GARDEN

Hebrew 12:2, 1 Peter 1:7

Becoming a Christian is the beginning of a journey. And like most journey's, you will find the road to be full of beautiful mountain peaks, and steep valleys. Throughout this journey it is important to hold onto Christ and His word.

Know that you will go through very difficult situations. Situations that; if you hold onto Christ, you will make it through. Remember, we are tried, so that the trying of our faith, while waiting on the Lord to deliver, builds our patience. There is so much growth in trials. And while it is difficult, painful, and you want out, if you hang in there, you will not only learn some wonderful things about yourself, you will be victorious in the end and you will be showing your love for Christ. You will also gain an appreciation of the things you already have even more so. Real love has to have an expression, as Jesus' love was expressed when He died for us. When we deal with the difficulties in life and don't abandon Christ, we show our love for Christ, our commitment to our walk, and our dedication to endurance.

36 EXPECT TO BE ATTACKED

Hebrew 11:13, 33, 39

It's difficult to accept being attacked verbally, or worse physically by others when you haven't done anything to deserve it. Yet, when you become a believer and you are growing, expect this to happen when you least deserve it. You will be hurt and wounded because these attacks will probably come from someone that you love.

Keep in mind when this is happening it means you are growing and this represents an opportunity to see if you *"got it"*. You consistency is being tested. These attacks are coming from those close to you because those you love are the ones that can hurt you the most. At times like this, study your word and pray so that you will overcome your own feelings of hurt and disappointment and understand what is actually going on. It is a spiritual battle that is raging.

37 EXPECT YOUR WAYS TO CHANGE

Proverb 24:21, 2 Corinthians 3:18

Once you become a believer, you will be *"convicted"* in your heart and mind about your behaviors and choices. No one has tell you to change, your spirit will not be comfortable with certain things, certain behaviors, certain styles of dress, and certain things will naturally drop off.

If you dress provocatively, you will begin to feel uncomfortable dressing this way and you will eventually change your mode of dress. While you can and should still be as stylish as you are comfortable with, you will find that dressing provocatively will no longer interest you. You will find that it is important that others see the God in you, not focus solely your own outer appearance. Remember, how you dress, what you say, how you carry yourself, tells the world about you.

You will also become uncomfortable with any form of gossip or negative talk. Your spirit will not be able to tolerate certain forms of music that doesn't uplift the spirit. Watch. It will gradually and automatically happen.

A word to long-time Christians: Be patient with new believers. Don't run them off with the *"rules"*. If the Lord has been patient with them this long, you can be patient with them for a little while longer. Trust me, the Lord is working on them as he did on you and he doesn't need your harsh help! Remember, your job is just to love them, share with them, and pray for them.

38 THE END IS COMING SOONER THAN YOU THINK

1 Thessolonians 4:16-17, Revelations 1:7

Prophesy is being fulfilled daily, the end is rapidly coming. Look at the situation in the Middle East. Investigate the work of the World Trade Organization and the United Nations, the move towards a one world government and cashless society. Consider the evil of Saddam Hussein and his current work of rebuilding the city of Babylon to its previous glory. Look at the simple clues in our everyday lives. The bible speaks of these events as signs of the end times. The computer and Internet have made it possible to communicate with everyone, everywhere, no matter what the language. We have rebuilt our tower of Babel.

It's important that we begin to study end time prophecy to see how close we are to the return of our Lord. There have been many great books published recently regarding the subject, like the *Left Behind* series and *Are We Living in End Times,* both by Dr. Tim LaHaye and Jerry Jenkins. There is no more powerful way to witness to others about Christ than showing how prophecy is being fulfilled in our world today.

39 FORGIVENESS WILL SET YOU FREE

Mark 11:25

How often have we held grudges against others for wrongdoing? Have you ever noticed that when you don't forgive others it stays in your heart and mind? You feel agitated and the wronged situation swirls around in your mind to the point that you are unable to focus on anything else? Your level of productiveness in developing your gifts becomes locked. Unforgiveness is destructive to your own physical being.

It is important to remember that when we forgive others, we release ourselves to move on. Forgiving others, even when they aren't repentant—when they don't acknowledge that they were wrong—is also important to your own well-being. Forgiveness is not just an act of saying "I forgive". It is forgiving with the heart. It is restoring that person to fellowship. It is when we release ourselves from the wounds inflicted by others and embrace that person back into the fold of love. Acceptance, fellowship, and relationship. Don't let the love in your heart be contaminated with unforgiveness. Forgiveness is about you—not them.

Real forgiveness isn't possible if we don't get out of *"our own selves"*—out of our *"feelings"*. We have to get into the spirit of Christ.

40 WE ARE ALL AT DIFFERENT PLACES IN CHRIST

2 Corinthians 3:18, 1 Peter 2:5

Everyone that comes into the knowledge of Christ comes with different curses that need to be overcome in their lives. Some are at ground zero. Some are not. Some of have greater faith than others. Despite these idiosyncrasy's, we are all loved and accepted by Christ.

As Christians, none of us are better or have arrived. We are all the righteous of God—moving along our journey of learning and growing at the unique pace that Christ is bringing us.

Lets remember to support all of our sisters and brothers in Christ in their journey. Let's encourage each other. Some of us are so new to the faith that basic things are not known. But be encouraged. The word is working, convicting them, and instructing them. Don't discourage and mock them. That's not our place.

41 LIKE A PARENT GOD WILL BLESS AND HE WILL DISCIPLINE

Deuteronomy 28:15-30

If we think of God like our parents, we will better understand His nature. Our Lord wants us to grow to be mature Christians. He wants us to walk in the spirit, not in our flesh (our feelings). He knows our growth will take some time and some hard times to get us to where we need to be. He extends His mercy when we ask for it because we are His children—when we are repentant in our hearts. But when we knowingly sin, He disciplines us for our own good

Our blessing or discipline is up to us. If we consistently walk in Gods word, fulfilling His mandates, we can be assured of His blessings. If we choose to be rebellious, discipline will soon follow. Just like our own children, when they are obedient, we bless them with privileges, things, etc. When they choose to be rebellious, discipline is on the horizon. As parents, the bible is clear on our responsibility to discipline. *"Foolishness is bound in the heart of a child, but the rod of correction shall drive it far from him,"* says Proverb 22:15.

Look at the children of Israel. Throughout their 40-year wandering they were constantly impatient and rebellious and God had to consistently discipline them. Our father doesn't enjoy disciplining us—that's why I believe he is so long suffering with us. He gives us every opportunity to turn things around, but when He doesn't see change, He has no other choice. Does this remind you of a parent's job?

42 IT IS ONLY A TEST

Isaiah 40:29-31

You've found the Lord. You're building a relationship. You're seeing blessings manifested in your life. Then, out of nowhere, POW! Just like that something major comes up that calls on you to sit back, trust God, and wait on Him for the outcome. Nothing you do changes the situation. Your only recourse is to pray and wait on God.

When you find yourself going through your 40 days and 40 nights, don't despair. It is only a test. When we are growing in Christ; what we have learned will be tested in our lives. God is trying your heart. If you have learned a lesson in forgiveness, count on having a situation crop up that will call for you to make a decision to forgive. During these difficult times God is teaching you that He is faithful. You learn His faithfulness through experience, not because you read it.

Our tests help our Lord see if we have truly put into practice what we claim to have learned. If we haven't truly learned our lesson, we can count on going through the test again and again, until we are able to put into practice, in practical ways in our lives and our heart, what we have learned.

43 LET YOUR MOUTH RULE
WITH KINDNESS

Matthew 15:11

The bible says the tongue is despitefully wicked. Our mouth creates the majority of the problems we have. We lie with it. We crucify others with it. It is considered quite a weapon.

When we don't rule our mouth, it can get away from us and cause destruction to our own life and the lives of others. We must always be conscious to use our mouth—our words—to encourage others, to build them up, to make them feel worthwhile.

This was an area in which I had a lot of work. I had a murderous mouth. I could destroy a person with words and was proud of it. I learned long ago that the best way to get revenge was not to physically hurt them, but to destroy them with words. A physical punch would hurt for a brief period of time, but a punch with words could potentially devastate them long-term. Foolishly I took pride in this until came into the full knowledge of God. I learned how this would hinder any closeness I would ever have with the Lord.

Since then I have become an encourager of others. My words are peppered with kindness. I no longer go after the jugular. Even when I'm provoked, the Holy Spirit helps keep me in check. While I'm not successful every time, my mouth is nowhere near the weapon it once was. Remember, kind words can be short and easy to speak, but their echoes are truly endless.

"Set a guard over my mouth, O Lord, keep watch over the door of my lips." Psalms 141:3

44 BE A PEACEMAKER

Matthew 5:9, 1 Corinthians 7:15

A peacemaker is one who wants peace at all cost. One who values it over being right or getting rewarded.

Are you a peacemaker? Do you yield your rightness in favor of peace or do you debate your point until you have buried your opponent? Often times we are right but the other party is so wrapped up in being right or getting the glory to the point of contention. If you find yourself in this situation, yield. The bible says, *"Blessed are the peacemakers for they shall be called the children of God"*, Matthew 5:19. In this walk, things are not easy. The response to the same situation in the world would be to stand your ground and fight for your position. But in Christ, we do the opposite. We don't fight the battle ourselves, we maintain our peace and let God deal with the situation.

Learn to be a peacemaker. The position is challenging, but the rewards are great.

45 LEARN TO BE FAITHFUL

Psalm 101:6-8, Luke 16:10-12

Are you faithful? Faithful is defined as loyal, worthy of trust, reliable. Being faithful says I can be counted on no matter what. Whatever you're faithful to is where your heart is. Sometimes we aren't really unfaithful, we just commit to doing things that we are unable to follow through on because we are over-scheduled. It makes us look unreliable.

We all get into the problem at one point or another. When you are asked to commit to working on a project, instead of committing right there. Let the person know you will get back to them. Then look at your current commitments. If you are unable to schedule the necessary time to do at least an adequate job, pass on it. It is better to let them know you are overscheduled, than to take it on and fail to follow through.

People don't care about your intentions. They care about what you actually do. We have to remember that broken commitments can become so repetitive and seemingly insignificant that they go unnoticed by the one breaking them.

46 BE CAREFUL ABOUT WHO YOUR TEACHERS ARE

Matthew 7:15-20

You must be careful and discriminating about where you accept input. Anyone can and are publishing books these days, but everyone is not an authority on their chosen topic. Be willing to study many sources yourself and come to your own conclusion. I include my own book in this. Take this book and study it against others of similar content, specifically the bible. Don't take anyone's word as law. Know for yourself.

A good example of this is in some churches. Some pastors will say *"half-truths"*, part scripture, part what sounds good. Too often a congregation will not do any independent study, assuming the pastor has studied and is correct, and the results: people led astray. Be careful with this. Because of this problem, many pastors today are backing the statements they make with scripture reference listed for your own independent study.

Remember, what you take in will impact your life—good or bad. It is up to you to choose reliable teachers that will add to your personal knowledge. No one has a neutral effect on you. Anyone you spend time with will have either a positive or negative effect on you. In the final analysis, it is your life. Be careful what you allow to be input. Just as knowledge is power, the lack of knowledge, or reliance upon misinformation is crippling, misleading, and harmful.

47 DON'T LIVE IN FEAR

Isaiah 35:4-, 2 Timothy 1:7

What are you afraid of? Not having enough money? Being alone? Being rejected. To some degree, we all fear something. The extent to which we overcome our fear depends on our ability to examine our fear and gain knowledge to help us overcome it. While a ship in a harbor is safe, that is not what ships are built for. Likewise, neither are we made to stay in safe places because of fear. Examine yourself. What is holding you back from doing what you should do? Why do you fear being alone? Is it because you haven't learned to appreciate your own company?

Take a moment to really look at your fears and find practical ways to overcome them. It is critical to your life success.

THE PARENT IN ME

48 PARENTING IS SERIOUS BUSINESS

I have always been amazed that we can become parents without the benefit of any training, but we must go through extensive questioning and a dry run to get a driver's license. Amazing! But I guess God figured we'd do it his way—teach our children as they were growing up—take it seriously. Unfortunately as time went on, parenting became a sideline instead of an important part of our life.

Parenting is hands down the most important job we can ever have. As a parent we are molding lives. We are shaping the minds and hearts of our future. What we give them or fail to give them will show up in the future of our society. Children's minds and hearts begin as blank pages—free of prejudices, pain, and insecurities. As life goes on and exposure to their life film moves along, our children get impacted by life's experiences. We either mold them into productive, healthy, spiritually confident individuals or they end up being individuals that are scarred in minor ways, or worse—they become unproductive, dependent individuals, lacking conscious and spiritual direction.

There is profound power in parenting. Parenting is not for children. By its very definition a parent gives of themselves in ways that many young people are incapable of doing. Parenting involves your time, your energy, your money, and all of your love. These apply—*even when you don't feel like it!* Being a real parent is a self-less act. A real parent will do without to ensure their children the very best opportunities. If you are not at this level, it's best not to have or keep a child.

Parenting is serious business. Ensure you are ready for it before you commit to children. Because once they're here, there's no turning back. If you're not prepared to properly care for a child, adoption is the best bet. While this is the next best option, there are a lot of children out there that aren't adopted and are living in group homes. No matter what you choose, if you're not ready to be a parent, don't become one, because everyone has the potential to lose.

49 STOP THE CURSE CALLED TEEN PREGNANCY

Were you a teen parent? Was your mother a teen parent? What about your father? Is your child now a teen parent? If you can say yes to at least two of these situations, your family is experiencing a "curse". A curse is something bad that repeats itself in the generations of a family. In this situation, the preceding generations believed through their actions that having sex without the benefit of marriage was acceptable, therefore having children without the benefit of marriage is okay. It is done with no thought of the powerful consequences it carries with it.

Stopping curses has to do with realizing that they exist, changing your mentality, and communicating that new mentality verbally and through your own actions to the next generation. If you tell your child not to have sex outside of marriage, it can't be just because it's wrong. It has to be wrong because of its consequences to their future.

We have to help our children find self-worth outside of the bedroom. And we can only do that if we demonstrate it to them. If our girls only see their single mothers looking for a man, and not doing what she needs to do to develop her own life as a single woman, then by our actions we are teaching our daughters that the most important thing is getting a man. Our children, especially our girls, have to get into their spirits that what they are telling a guy when they agree to have sex with them without the benefit of commitment is *"I'm not very important. I'm not worth your best and my love isn't good enough"*. We send that message every time we open our legs and unzip our pants without the benefit of commitment. It's that simple. We have to learn, *then* teach, our children the difference between love and lust. Lust gets. Love gives. Love also waits. If we as adults haven't learned these truths, we have to be honest with ourselves, learn, and apply the truth that we've learned to our own lives. Then, in a very open way, let our children know (because they already know) how wrong we were, and begin anew from there, showing, instead of telling, how to live.

50 IF YOU ARE A TEEN PARENT: WHAT NOW?

If you are a teen parent, don't lose hope. I was a teen parent, and with the moral support of my family; my daughter and I were okay. I was fortunate because my dad understood it was too late to destroy me verbally because of it. He understood he had to get geared up to help me be the best parent I could be. He, my grandmother, and my sister, helped guide me in my role. They took on roles, but didn't remove my responsibility as a parent. I worked to support my daughter and myself. I changed my mentality. I had to transition from thinking like a teen to thinking like an adult. While her father pulled a "hit and run", I was fortunate to have wonderful role models for her in friends and family.

While this is a very serious, very traumatic time, remember you can and will survive it. If you are currently in this situation, look for my next book, *Surviving Teen Pregnancy: Important Skills You'll Need to Navigate Your Way to Success*. It will provide more details on what you can do to turn your life around and head down the road to your own success.

51 MAKE TIME FOR YOUR MATE

You are saddled with a job, children, cooking, cleaning, kids activities, extended family, and elderly parents. By weeks end you are run down and ready for a peaceful rest. You don't want one more person to ask you to do one more thing! But in all the activity of the week, you have barely spoken to your spouse, let alone had any real intimate time to connect.

We live in a fast pace society, filled with a variety of worthwhile and entertaining things to do. There is rarely any down time. Most couples have a rough time making time to spend time alone together. This can be dangerous. By not making the time to spend time together to bond, we open the door for problems, and possibly infidelity.

As a couple, you must make time to spend together alone. Time to regroup and reconnect. While you may not be able to leave town for a weekend bed and breakfast, you can both decide not to work as hard. To get home by a certain time, put the kids to bed early, close out the world—no phone, no television— just the two of you.

If you have a crazy, hectic schedule like most couples, plan a date to do this at least once every month. Making the time for each other will take your relationship far in ensuring you have a relationship that endures.

There are many inexpensive things you can do to spend time alone like, having a picnic at the beach or at the park or simply walking along the beach together, talking and sharing—an activity that allows you to focus on each other. The purpose is to spend some non-sexual time together. I have always been a very sexual person. Always wanting that time to include the intimacy of lovemaking. While my husband also enjoys lovemaking, he taught me the importance of putting sex aside so we could focus on each other. This has added a new element to our relationship and the anticipation in waiting has made our lovemaking more exciting.

Take time to invest in your relationship. Keep in mind, dishes can wait, cleaning can wait, but building relationships can't.

52 YOUR TEENS NEED YOUR TIME

We spend a great deal of time with our children, but what we consider spending time is actually time spent in passing—running them to activities, reviewing homework, etc. We don't actually *spend* time with them. When was the last time you had lunch with your child—just the two of you at a restaurant? When was the last time you all sat and watched a television show or video together? Or sitting down talking with them before they go to bed?

There are so many ways we can spend time with our children. When we spend the time with them, we get to know them. We get to know their hopes and dreams. We get to share with them how we were at their age. And if we are honest, they will sometimes reveal their true selves to us. This private time is time of openness and sharing. It is not time of conviction or blame. It is in these times that we develop the open channel of communication that will help us when serious matters demand that we have a level of communication with our children.

Take time every week to draw your child out and communicate with them. It's important to your relationship with them, and to the future communication you will need to have with them.

53 BRING UP A CHILD IN THE WAY IT SHOULD GO

The bible says bring up a child in the way it should go and when it is old it will not depart from it. One of the reasons that our society is in its current state is due to our lack of bringing up children in the way they should go. What does that mean? It means following the moral rules established in the bible. Our principles and laws of our country are based in scripture. As parents we have a responsibility to instill in our children the importance of "how they should go—or how they should behave", and the consequences of failing to do so.

54 DON'T OVERKILL WITH ACTIVITIES

We are a society filled with a variety of activities. Basketball, baseball, soccer, dance classes, church activities, and on and on. We run our children to and from activities, involving them in a variety of activities to keep them out of trouble. In the race to keep them out of trouble, we are burning them, and out selves, out. They are left with no time to be kids.

Being a kid used to be a simple time—playing ball outside, skateboarding, going to the park to hang out with friends. Today's kids have no "hang out" unplanned time. We need to ensure that with busy schedules, our children, like ourselves, have unscheduled time to do "nothing". They need to have time to do the things they like to do.

Each child is different and each child has a different need for more flexibility, so talk with your child, look for burnout because of overwhelming activities. Children will have to grow up soon enough. Don't rush the process.

55 BE PATIENT WITH THE LITTLE ONES: THEY ARE LEARNING

I have to be reminded of this daily. My granddaughter is now 7-years-old and full of energy. She literally runs until she is exhausted. Because of this she can wear out any grownup. Full of questions and conversation, she absorbs a great deal of what is presented to her. While her great surge of energy, enthusiasm, conversations and questions frustrate me, all this activity is her way of learning. She is a kinetic child. She learns through touching, moving, and talking.

As parents and grandparents, we have to be aware of the unique ways of learning for each individual. We must understand and accept these and encourage the learning process. As busy adults, this isn't always easy, but necessary it is.

56 WE LEARN BY WHAT WE SEE, NOT NECESSARILY BY WHAT IS SAID

If you have ever watched a toddler play, you'll see the great importance setting an example plays in the lives of human beings. Toddlers watch intensely what you do and they mimic the actions. As a whole, this is how we all learn. As a child grows, they not only take the action you do, they match it with what you say. If the two conflict, you will not only lose their respect, they will still follow what you do.

It's important to remember, we lead by example. How you live tells people who you are and what you believe far more than what you say. When you make a conscious decision to live out what you say you believe, you will ultimately see the results in your children.

57 LEARN THE ART OF DELAYED GRATIFICATION

We are a hurry up society. We want it and we want it right now! We are so into satisfying our desires that we will go into debt to get that high. Delayed gratification helps us to strike an importance balance in our lives. It teaches us the importance of waiting and not being impetuous. This is important to learn ourselves and to pass along to our children. When we help our children learn to wait until we can afford what we want, their appreciation level for it is greater because they had to save for it. It didn't come because WE had the money. It came because they waited until THEY had enough. When they learn to wait, their level of appreciation is increased.

Take a moment today and think of ways in your everyday life that you can learn and teach this valuable lesson.

58 BLENDED FAMILIES CAN WORK IF YOU'RE WILLING TO WORK

With the skyrocketing divorce and remarriage rates, children of single mothers, children born to teen parents; blended families have become the norm. Stepparents and step children are more common today than they were just 25 years ago.

Stepparents and stepchildren sometimes have a difficult time of it. It is normal for children to have allegiances to their natural parents. It is also normal for them to have the fantasy of their parents reuniting the family. Likewise it is normal for parents to have a greater bond with their own child over someone else's child.

But when you make the decision to commit to someone else that has a child by a previous relationship in which the other parent is alive and available, expect to have a period of adjustment. This adjustment period can vary based on the history of the previous relationship and the relationships with the children. If you are a stepparent, don't move in and assert authority with the other children. If you don't have that type of relationship developed with the child you have to wait until a relationship of respect is established. In the meantime, let the natural parent handle the discipline or other sensitive areas. You just be a friend.

If you are the parent with a child in the home: remember to watch for unfair behavior from both your child and your spouse, and remember to be sensitive in the way you handle it. You will be the one responsible for keeping the peace with your children in your new home. With time, patience, and sensitivity, the bond of your new family will get established.

If you are a child in this situation: while you may be upset and disappointed in your parents, remember, they have a right to find workable relationships. As long as your natural parents do all they can to be supportive of each other and of you, you have a responsibility to work within the framework of this new family. Doing all you can to make things work will go far in securing your future happiness.

59 BE CONSISTENT

Too often we say things we don't follow through on or make threats we know we don't mean. When we do this, we damage our credibility with our children. When we are faced with making decisions, take a moment to truly think about what you want to say. Think about what degree of consequence you really mean to follow through on. Then make sure you follow through on it!

Our children need consistency. They need to know what the boundaries are and only you can establish these for them.

60 ITS OKAY TO BE WRONG IF YOU'RE WILLING TO ADMIT IT

Many parents hate to be wrong to the point of not admitting when they are. Our children are bright, savy people. When we are wrong and won't admit our wrongness, it frustrates them and teaches them to lie to save their own pride, to keep them from embarrassment.

We must remember the importance of helping our children become well-rounded individuals that realize they don't have all the answers and they will not always be right—no one will.

61 BE A PARENT AND A FRIEND

Many of us were taught that we are not our children's friends, we are their parents only. Well, we are our children's parents, and sometimes we have to make that point perfectly clear. Then there are other times when they need our understanding. They need us to be their friend. They need to confide a wrong without being destroyed for it.

I remember when my daughter's friend shared with me that she was sexually active. I was so hurt. Not only because she was sexually active, but because she didn't feel comfortable enough to come to me. She didn't perceive me as a friend, so she couldn't confide in me. There are critical times like these when our children need us to be a friend.

We must learn to give them advice and not be so shocked at the question or thoughts or confessions that we can't address them in sensible and sensitive ways.

62 YOUR CHILDREN ARE INDIVIDUALS—DON'T COMPARE THEM

I remember growing up being compared to my sister. She was so neat and fastidious. At the time I couldn't be neat if you paid me to be. I admired how she kept her clothes in perfect order—color-coded, by long sleeves to short sleeves—everything perfect. It was wonderful to look at. My dad always reminded me of my sister's habit of neatness whenever he saw a mess in my room. "Why couldn't I be more like her?", was his constant statement to me. I didn't like the comparison because it told me I wasn't good enough on my own. I had to be like her to be acceptable.

Later in life I found I was doing the same things to my children. Once I realized that I was bringing this same "curse".

63 ENSURE YOUR CHILDREN DEMONSTRATE BASIC LIFE SKILLS BEFORE THEY LEAVE HOME

Our world is a lot more complicated than it used to be. There is so much more we need to know to be successful after we leave our parents home. It's important that our children demonstrate basic life skills before leaving our home to live on their own. Some practical skills to know: How to balance a check book, how to prepare at least three different breakfasts, lunches and dinners, How to file taxes, how to handle car registration, and something as basic as how to locate getting around the town they live in by the bus if it becomes necessary.

Teaching them the basics allows them not only to be prepared for the future, but allows for delegating chores and other responsibilities around the house. They learn and you have help. Learning basic life skills will go far in assisting our children in surviving in the world without making mistakes because of lack of knowledge. You can begin teaching basics as early as three years old. Children that age can learn how to return things to their place, take out light trash cans, etc.

64 GIVE THEM THE GIFT OF
A CLOSE FAMILY

I never really understood the importance of a close family until I got married. My husband has five brothers and a sister and a host of nieces and nephews. Despite the fact that they don't always agree, and can sometimes be catty and petty with one another, they have mastered the art of true closeness and commitment to one another. Despite their hurts and conflicts, they get over it, move on, and maintain their closeness. I'd never seen anything like it before. After brutally painful words hurled at each other, they could come back a few minutes later to plan meeting for a movie and dinner later that evening.

My family was not like this. If we had a blowout—forget it. You are banished to Syberia and the other party would not only ignore you, they would recruit and encourage other family members to talk about you and ignore you as well. The result of this is that cousins, nieces and nephews never get to be close to uncles or aunts or each other.

I have learned how destructive this behavior is to everyone in the family. It is important to remember we all have "stuff" to deal with. No one is perfectly right in what they say or how they do things. Everyone has areas they need to grow in. The important thing is maintaining the family relationships. We can't and shouldn't try to throw away family. Family should be the haven you go to when there is nowhere else to go. Family should have your back, they should love you even when you blow it and they don't agree with you. As family members we are to tell the truth, in love, but love and encourage you just the same. Don't just throw criticisms, find something good that person does and encourage them in that area, then show concern for the area that needs improvement.

I have learned the love of a real family has healing properties. While family can sometimes be the most brutal, family should be your lifeline back from hell.

If your family has fractured relationships, take time today to recognize the beauty and importance of family. Honor and cherish it, and you'll be surprised at the life time rewards it will bring.

65 STAY IN TOUCH WITH EXTENDED FAMILY

→

It's not always easy to stay close to extended family, but it's very possible to stay in contact. Your extended family—uncles, aunts, great aunts, etc., have very important roles in the lives of your children, passing along the history of your family.

We are all blessed with a rich heritage. Family interwoven with the rich traditions and the present and past generations. The many marriages that entwine other families, other cultures, other places that make our family uniquely our own.

Even if you call or just email once a month, make the time to show your extended family their importance to you. Not only will you benefit, but your family will be galvanized to do the same and you're entire family will feel the connectedness we all look for.

66 INTRODUCE THEM TO YOUR FAITH

No matter what your spiritual beliefs, it's important to introduce the basic and tenents of your faith to your children early.

Young children are like sponges. They absorb almost all of what is taught to them and maintain curious minds. They are pliable and receptive to what you communicate and demonstrate. No other time in life is a person this receptive in their spirit. As a parent you want to root your children in the fundamentals of your faith so as they grow through life, they can experience the truth of what is taught.

While some things seem ritualistic, the very act of going to church, temple, or whatever your place of worship is, reciting faith based stories, remembering the Passover and Resurrection Sunday should not just be fluff holidays about a man called Santa Claus and an Easter bunny.

Sharing your faith with your children doesn't guarantee they will always keep your faith as theirs, but it will give them a foundation of truth that will be hard to destroy when they become adults.

67 PASS ALONG FAMILY STORIES AND HEIRLOOMS

My grandmother had a beautiful silver wedding ring set. The rings, reminiscent of estate jewelry, were entrusted to my sister. Upon my grandmothers death, the sunburst quilt she hand made from the strips of leftover cloth now adorns the bed of my father. At my wedding, my eldest sister gifted me with the china tea cup my mother enjoyed her morning coffee in.

All of these objects, while worthless to others, represent priceless mementos for us. Each of these mementos evoke memories that soften the past. They help us find pleasure in remembering a certain moment or experience with that person. They also help us heal hurts of past conflicts. Our family stories and heirlooms help establish a sense of worth for the one who holds them, as well as a sense of continuity.

In biblical times the family head passed on "the blessing" to the first born. "The blessing" signified God's favor and dealing with the first born. Not only this, each child was left an "inheritance" of the material wealth from that family. While we still do this today to some degree, the importance of heirlooms of significance to specific individuals should not be forgotton.

The passing on of heirlooms should be from generation to generation. Each generation adding something of importance of their own to pass along. Think of important items you can pass along to your sons and daughters. What about an important piece of jewlry that carries an unusual story with it? Or something as simple as a polished shell found on a beach during a turbulent time in your life that signified how everything and everyone goes through transition and renewal?

Give these items only at appropriate times and at appropriate ages of responsibility. A sixteen year old that doesn't demonstrate a responsibe nature should not be given a grandmother's engagement ring. Wait until they can appreciate the special significance of the heirloom. This will ensure to have the right impact and will maintain the value of the item.

Family stories are also important to pass along. Most of the problems our youth face today is because the lack of understanding the positive contributions of the past by their own family. They simply don't know who they are.

Share the stories of our lives with our children and grandchildren. They need to know about your grandmother that sold eggs to make her way to California for a better life for her family. They need to know about the uncle that went to prison, came out turned his life around, and is now a successful businessman. These stories, along with biblical truths, can help instill the values in your children in very meaningful ways.

68 USE TOUGH LOVE IF NECESSARY

I recently heard someone say tough love is removing love. But I'd have to disagree. Whether we realize it or not tough love is the kind of live God uses on us. It is never used as a first resort (remember the importance of long suffering). But when you've done you're best. When you've done all you can, and you don't see improvement, there is no other choice.

Tough love is more about handing the situation over to God. It is about removing responsibility for that person and making them responsible for their actions. In tough love you don't rescuer them from the messes they create. You advise them if they are open to it, and you leave them to make a way out of it.

Love in its very definition is not the giving of things—love is giving of your heart and soul. It is about encouragement. Things become a by-product of love. Giving things of itself isn't love.

God demonstrates tough love for us every day to all of us who choose to live in disobedience. He tries every avenue available until he see's no other alternative but to pull back his resources until you see no other way, recognize who He is and decide to return to Him.

We have to be careful not to get so caught up in supporting bad behavior that we fail to see God's examples in the bible and in life everyday. Again, we are here for a purpose uniquely our own and God expects growth in us a He would from a fruit tree. A fruit tree that doesn't bare fruit is useless—when it doesn't function in its purpose, it is destroyed (scripture).

Look at those around you. Do you need to start some tough love? Is it time to take a stand, in love, and begin to gradually remove responsibility for a loved one caught in the whirlwind of laziness? There are many capable people using crutches to keep from being responsible for their own lives. What are the crutches we hold ourselves up with? "No one will hire me" or "That's not what I really want to do". When you kick the crutch from under a capable person, they (and you) are usually surprised at how well they can stand on their own. But as long as the crutch is there, there is no incentive to stand. Think about it.

69 REQUIRE SOMETHING
OF YOUR CHILDREN

Our children are basking in a wealth of material things without learning some of the expectations life will have of them. Kids are getting cars, computers, games, all the trappings of entertainment, but we re requiring very little of them to have it.

There was a time when we would have to work all summer just to get money for that cherished bike. And when we got what we worked for, we took great care of it. We didn't indiscriminately lend it out because we knew what it took for us to get it. Today our children don't have that same appreciation level for things because it takes little beyond asking to get it. Yes, we do live in different times. And maybe we want our children to have more than we had when we were growing up. But it's still important that our children learn to earn those things they say they want. If you son wants a $150 pair of Jordan basketball shoes, if you are purchasing them and he is not putting in money for them, require extra things of him around the house, and be specific.

70 SAY WHAT YOU MEAN
AND MEAN WHAT YOU SAY

How often have you said things like, "You'd better clean your room or you'll never get to play basketball again!" or something similar? We make idle threats all the time to our children. And when they don't follow through, as they should, we don't follow through with the threatened action. Of course you won't kill your child for a minor infraction, but that's what we threaten.

To be effective in getting the results we want, we must remember to make consequences reasonable things that we will follow through and do. We must say what we mean and mean what we say. This also applies when we commit to do something for them or with them. Take the time to think before you commit to doing something. Canceling out later will cause you to look unreliable if you make it a habit.

Our children need to be able to count on us. If you can't do what they want you to do, be honest, upfront, and commit to doing something another time. How many children have fathers outside of the home that say "I'm coming to see you this weekend", and they never call and never show up?

When we fail to follow through for them we are telling them they are not important enough to us. If our children can count on anyone, it should be us. We owe them that.

71 SPEND FAMILY TIME TOGETHER

Our society is so fast paced that we rarely have time to actually spend time together. With activities, friends, and other commitments, not to mention television and the internet, we've lost the fine art of conversation and no longer really know each another, let alone our children.

We need to commit to making time each week to spend time with just "our family". Because of schedules—sports activities, work, school, its difficult to make the time. But my family makes time at least twice per week for time together. Sometimes we watch sports together, sometimes we have dinner together. Often we will all—my son, my husband, and myself,—we will get on our knees and say nightly prayers with our granddaughter. She is five-years-old and this has become a very important, very comforting ritual for her. Not only has she benefited from this, as a family this has been a time of closeness and support for us all. It has bonded us in our faith as well as in our relationships. Sometimes our son will come in the room and just "hang out" with us. During these times he'll share things that are going on in his life—with his friends, at school—and during this sharing if he receives a phone call from a friend, he declines the call; letting them know he'll call them back 'cause he's talking to his parents. When he does this, it makes me realize how important this time is to him.

When our children realize they have an open door to spend time with us, and when we provide an open environment for them, the usually will spend the time. Sometimes you may be tired. Sometimes you may want to put it off. But make the time.

MISCELLANEOUS

72 BLOOM WHERE YOU ARE PLANTED

Look at where you are. What can you do today to make it better? Where you are is proving ground for where you want to go. If you want to be a counselor, are you counseling those in your immediate environment? How successful are you at that? Mastering where you are will automatically expand your base, and ultimately take you where you want to go. To succeed, do the best you can, where you are, with what you have.

The lure of the distant and different is sometimes deceptive. The great opportunity is where you are.

73 EVERY ACTION HAS A REACTION

My grandmother used this statement all the time. It was true in day and still is today. We have to learn to carefully weigh our decisions. Every decision will positively or negatively impact our lives today, in years to come, and will usually impact the lives of others close to us as well. Everyone will experience the consequences of his own acts. If his acts are right, he'll get good consequences, if they're not, he'll suffer for it. Failures are divided into two classes—those who thought and never did, and those who did and never thought.

Look at the pros and cons of all major decisions in your life. Ask someone you trust for advice. Better yet, pray. At some point in your life you will have to make a serious life altering decision. Remember to consider the ramifications down the line before you commit, because when you choose the behavior you choose the consequence.

74 NO PITY PARTIES, PLEASE

Do you spend a great deal of time and energy feeling sorry for yourself? You're unhappy with your appearance? Your husband doesn't pay enough attention to you, and such complaints? **Get over it!** When we expend energy on being wounded by others behavior, we pull ourselves away from our productive, creative place and get locked into focusing on *"self"*. Again, we need to release our focus on *"self"* and our feelings and focus on the task at hand. When you're busy with your creative pursuits, you'll find you won't have time for pity parties. Reduce pity parties by focusing on the following: Attitude—Don't let anyone or anything conquer you. Agenda—Prioritize your day. Action—Take action on what you put on your agenda. Associate—be careful whom you associate with. Learn how to discern between negative and positive people.

In the final analysis, most people don't care about your complaints and the rest are glad it's you and not them.

75 WHAT YOU EXPECT IS WHAT YOU GET

There is tremendous power in what you think and what you speak. What you meditate on in your mind is the beginning of what will come into existence in your life. How often have you said, *"I think I'm getting sick",* then you began to get the full-blown sickness? When you agreed with what you body is feeling, then backed it up with your talk, you ultimately manifested it into being. When you choose the thought you choose the consequences.

This principle works in reverse as well. If you want more joy in your life, be joyful. If you want more peace in your life, be peaceful. Whatever you truly want, expect it, and gradually the wind of expectation will blow it your way.

76 PERFORMANCE AND PERCEPTION ARE EVERYTHING

What you do and how you are thought of speaks volumes. It has been said that we subconsciously make a judgment of others within the first five minutes of meeting them. While this is not always fair, it is something that is so subconscious that we don't normally realize it. Our perceptions of others are usually based on previous experiences with others that exhibit like behavior. If a dog has bitten you, you probably have a negative perception of dogs. If you were ripped-off by a used car salesman, you probably have a negative perception of used car salesmen. Conversely, if you received great treatment at a certain department store, you will have a positive perception of the whole chain.

Make it a priority to always do your best. Go above and beyond. Others take note to this and you will stand out. This applies to everything you do—in your job, with your family, in your community activities, etc. Resolving that you will require excellence from yourself is a defining moment. Remember, we are what we repeatedly do. Excellence, then, is not an act but a habit.

77 HANG IN THERE

You are running late for work, your child is sick, you have a project deadline due today, you're not getting along with your sister so your heart is heavy, your husband is being demanding, and you have a run in your pantyhose! You are going through it! While you may be tempted to throw in the towel, just hang in there! Realize there will be many forces at work to throw you off course. Children acting up, family issues, and well meaning friends can sometimes throw a hitch in your plans. Remember, the difference between a successful person and the others is not a lack of strength, not a lack of knowledge, but rather a lack of will. Stay focused.

78 LEARN TO PUT UP WITH SOME DISCOMFORT

It is necessary to have discomfort to truly appreciate our blessings. Struggle is a decided advantage, because it develops those qualities, which would forever lie dormant without it. When the winds of adversity come your way, steer your way through them until you get to the other side. Your worth, your character will not be known in the easy moments of your life. It will show itself clearly in a crisis. No life is exempt from hard times, because life is a series of mountains and valleys. Based on our need to learn we will be in one or the other.

This principle applies not only to our own lives, but also to the lives of our children. We have a tendency to make things easy to the point of expecting little or nothing from them. It's important that they learn the value of winning, but also losing, the value of comfort, as well as discomfort. No one ever has blue skies everyday. We cripple our children if we don't prepare them for the difficult times in life. Through difficulty, our children will learn their true worth and will ultimately achieve the integrity and character we desire them to acquire.

Despite discomfort, we have to be willing to run through the hard and painful stuff. We have to learn not to quit. Not to let discomfort end our quest. We can endure to the end or fall by the wayside. It's totally up to us.

79 PICK YOUR BATTLES

There are many battles to fight in our lives. Some important: some not so important. Do we repeatedly argue with our children about cleaning up behind themselves or do we get firm with our children about the friend that is a troublemaker? Obviously, we stand our ground about the troublemaker-friend. That *"friend"* has the potential to carry your child down a terribly wrong road. While we would *'like it"* if they were neater, in the larger equation, a neat room isn't the end all.

We don't have to fight every battle in our life. Fight only those that go against your core values or those battles that threaten the future of you or your family. Your core values are those areas that are life and death to you. If it doesn't fit in this *core value or threatening"* category, try reasoning, or just work around it. Life is too complicated to go to the mattresses for something insignificant. Peace and fellowship are more important and most insignificant things work themselves out over time.

80 BE SPECIFIC

Often times we are not specific in our wants and needs. We assume others know exactly what we want, what we're asking for. We are generally disappointed when we approach life from this way. It is important to remember that we all perceive things based on our experiences, and therefore bring different conclusions to a particular situation. Most often when things are not done the way you want them to be done, it is more a lack of understanding specifically what you want or how you want something done.

Be specific in what you want and what you ask for. If you want your children to clean their room, be specific. Tell them I want you to make up your bed, clean under your bed, dust your dresser, hang up your clothes, etc. Give them specifics; SHOW them how to do those things the way you want them done. Ensure they understand exactly what you're expecting. That way, if they don't follow through, it was a choice not to—it wasn't because they didn't understand. This system applies with everyone in every situation, at all times. When we are clear and specific, we generally get the results we want.

81 DEVELOP YOUR SPIRITUAL SELF

Those that have not looked into the spiritual nature of their lives are probably still trying to find that elusive *"completion"* in their lives. We look to *"if I had more money"*, or *"if I had a larger house"*, *"if I had a husband"*, we look to so many things, but we make looking to God the last resort, if we look there at all.

During the course of my life I have met and befriended all kind of folks—both wealthy and poor, and the one thing I have learned is being spiritually empty—not looking at the spiritual side of life, not growing in this area—is to truly be poor. You can have it all—money, possessions, but without beginning that journey to spiritual growth, you will always long for something to make your life complete. Something will always be missing.

82 YOU WILL REAP WHAT YOU SOW

"…*Whatever a man soweth, that shall he also reap.*"(Gal.6: 7, KJ). This is
a natural principle of life. Whatever you put out there you get back. If you
put out love, you will get it back. If you circulate your wealth, you will grow
your wealth. This also works in reverse. If you put out hate, you will receive
hate. If you're negative, negative will surround you. You get what you give.
Also, don't ask people to do what you are not willing to do yourself.

Look at your life. What is the dominant thing you see? Do you see your life
surrounded with friends? If so, you have been a friend. Whatever you want in
abundance in your life, DO in abundance and you will reap the rewards.

83 HONOR YOUR BOUNDARIES AND THOSE OF OTHERS

This is an unspoken rule of life. Most of us know what limit we should go with others. Like how long we should stay at a party, how long we should be a houseguest, returning things borrowed from someone else. Most of us know this stuff in our hearts, but too often we ignore it because it is not convenient for us. It is important to respect the boundaries of others. Some boundaries are common sense and unspoken. If boundaries have not been established and you are unclear, ask that person.

Likewise we need to honor our own boundaries. If we do things for others and complain about it later, we have overstepped our own boundaries—doing what we are not comfortable doing. When you get yourself into this fix, don't say, *"Why are they doing this to me?"* Begin saying *"Why am I doing this to myself?"* As a rule, you are not respecting your own boundaries if you are not happy helping someone. What behaviors and choices can you change to get a different result?

If you are uncomfortable doing something for someone, simply let them know, *"I'm sorry, but I cannot help you at this time,"* or *"I'm not comfortable doing this particular thing."* You don't have to explain beyond this and you don't have to make excuses.

CAREER

84 EVERY ABLE BODY SHOULD CONTRIBUTE

If you are living, breathing and functional, you should contribute to your environment. Environment is defined as where you live and/or where you work. You might say why would I say that about someone who goes to work? Simply because some people *go* to work, but don't really *contribute* as they should. They either go and hang out, socializing, or they do the minimum to get them through the day.

Everyone has a responsibility to contribute to this life. If you live in a home, you have a responsibility to contribute to that home in whatever way you can. If you don't work outside the home and don't earn an income, you can contribute by assisting in maintaining the home. Take out the trash, wash dishes, vacuum the floors, clean windows, do laundry, or cook meals. If you only have a small amount in the way of finances, contribute by offering to pay a gas bill, or contribute to the phone bill (you use it, don't you?).

Whatever way you can contribute, do so. When you show that you are a responsible person, you will be treated as a responsible person, and you will find doors opening up to you. When you contribute positively to your environment, others will contribute to your life in a positive manner. Again, you reap what you sow.

If you allow others to live in your home without expecting some sort of contribution, you not only get used, you hurt them by stunting their growth. Without providing expectation, there is no hope for their growth. Help is just that—help. It is not to be a continual thing without end. Whether we realize it or not, our life is about service, and when we come to that realization, only then will we begin to grow.

85 PRAY, PLAN, PREPARE, POSITION, AND TO GET WHERE YOU WANT TO GO

This is potentially the key to success. Plan purposefully, prepare prayerfully, proceed positively, and pursue persistently. When you accomplish all the above, you have covered all the bases. Lets break it down and begin with what is probably the most often ignored—that is to pray. Everyone doesn't have the same spiritual beliefs that I have, but I cannot ignore this one. Everyone should believe in a higher power than himself or herself—a God that is all knowing and has all wisdom. In this world we see things as either worldly or spiritual. Unfortunately the secular world does things from a practical place and doesn't consider the spiritual vantage point. And the church does things from a spiritual place, but often ignores practicality. When the spiritual and the practical are fused together, expect to see powers manifested.

At the beginning of your planning, preparing and positioning, pray for direction. God put us here for His purpose and if we pray, He will definitely direction our way. *"A man's mind plans his way, but the Lord directs his steps."* (Proverb 16:9).

Next you need to develop a plan: What do you want to do with your life? What are you good at? What are your interests? What is your passion? Once you reach an answer to the above, the next step is to make a plan. Plan out a route to get to that destination. Begin by writing down your goals in detail. The difference between a goal and a dream is that a goal is mapped out on paper. A path is established to help you get there—both long term and short-term goals, along with a completion date. With today's information age you can get information on anything at all, anytime. But you have to be willing to do the work. If you don't have a computer, most libraries do and have the staff there to help you research the Internet on any career path you want to take. It's up to you.

Next you need to prepare. Preparation has to do with getting the education you need to fulfill the requirements of the career you are seeking. Do you need to go to a 4-year college? Will a 2-year junior college or trade school do? Whatever it is you say you want to do, you have to fulfill the preparation phase, no matter how good you are at it. A singer needs to take singing lessons. While she may have a gift for singing, there are things you learn by taking lessons that may take her to another level, help her prepare better. The secret of success in life is to be ready for opportunity when it comes. Not only is preparation necessary, the proper training in the necessary arena brings you to the next step, which is position.

Positioning oneself is important. Often times who you know is as important as what you know. Through preparation you will find that you will meet people in your desired industry and they can be conduits to that first job.

86 DO WHAT YOU LOVE, NOT WHAT OTHERS EXPECT

This is especially for young adults transitioning into the adult world of responsibility. By your sophomore year in high school, you should at least have some idea where you want to take your life, because your grades and extracurricular activities should be in line with what you want to do.

Too often we are caught looking only at what our parents and teachers say we should do. Now, if you don't have any specific things you are passionate about doing, by all means listen to them. They have watched your life and are aware of your gifts and talents and will be valuable in directing you on a course towards a workable career.

On the other hand if you have a career goal that you have a passion for, go for it. Dale Carnegie said it beautifully, *"To be happy, set yourself a goal that commands your thoughts, liberates your energy, and inspires your hopes"*. Remember, if your goals conflict with those primary adults that support you, you need to find reasonable arguments to support why you want to do it, and SHOW them your plans towards reaching this goal. If they continue to resist you, you may have to forgo it until you are supporting yourself financially. When you stand on your own two feet—support yourself financially—you have greater decision-making power. Most parents will get behind you if you have mapped out your plans in a way that they can visualize, no matter how creative the goal.

Either way, once you begin to listen to yourself and God's plan for your life, you will see that other people's answers do NOT always work for you. The word of God always whispers to the willing mind. Once you discover your direction and purpose in life, it is difficult and painful to do anything else. Once you embrace your purpose, the Lord will bring you down the path.

The hardest thing you ever do, may be the greatest thing you ever do.

87 DON'T LOSE SIGHT OF YOUR PRIORITIES

We lead lives that clearly show why we lose sight of our priorities. Intense careers, and many other things pulling at our time. By the time we get home, complete the chores, review the homework, prepare dinner, organize for the next day, we have nothing left to invest. A good friend of mine once said, "*We use our talents for our jobs, but we fail to use some of them to lift our lives to the level we want them to be.*" This is so true.

I had made my priority to write this book. This book has actually taken me five years to write, only because I allowed all of life's events to take precedence. True, I had a lot to deal with: health issues, deaths in the family, changes on my job, but still, a little work everyday could have gotten this book done in less than a year. I lost sight of my priorities. When I realized what I had done, I purposed that I would give myself a deadline, commit time each day to my priorities, while letting go some of my involvement in things that hindered my progress. While some of the things I was involved with were worthwhile, they did not bring me closer to completing what was a priority for me, so I had to let them go.

Take some time to list those things that are important for you to do. Also list those things that you have to do; like taking care of your family, meeting the needs of elderly parents. Once you've completed your list look at what you can release from your list. Then, release yourself from those responsibilities. Releasing yourself from doing for others is difficult because they generally won't let you do it easily. But keep in mind; it is necessary if you want to succeed.

88 DON'T FORGET TO GIVE BACK AND PULL UP

➤

You've made it. You're where you always dreamed you would be. Now, remember to share the information, extend encouragement to those who are truly interested in moving forward as well. It is a responsibility that we all have to help someone else survive what we have endured. There is true fulfillment in helping others.

This principle was played out for me when I got serious about this project. My sister-in-law graciously extended a wealth of information and introduced me to many of her friends in the writing field and they did the same. No one took the attitude that we we're in competition and they couldn't help me. With the information and encouragement I received from this special group of individuals, I was able to complete this project.

We all need others. And remember you reap what you sow. Again. This is an important principle of nature. As you prosper, assist others in prospering.

89 EDUCATION IS THE KEY

This is a different world now than it was when I was growing up. When I was coming up you could get a decent job with a large company. You could get paid medical benefits, established company matching retirement accounts, and paid vacations. While these things are still available, these jobs are going to those who have education beyond high school. These days you have to have a college degree or some additional training in specialized fields.

Our world has changed dramatically within my lifetime. A four-year college isn't necessarily the answer, but additional training is. There are specialized trade schools that give you the needed credentials within a year.

Even after you have attained a position with a company or started your own company, continuing education is key to staying competitive in your industry. This is the information age—take advantage of it or get left behind.

You will discover that in life, you can only go as far as your faith, wisdom, and knowledge will take you. Think about it: Who is more foolish: A child afraid of the dark, or a man afraid of the light?

90 NO JOB IS BENEATH YOU

When I was growing up my grandmother taught my sister and I lessons that stick with me to this day. One of the most profound lessons she ever taught us was the importance of taking pride in doing the very best in everything that we attempted to do. Whether that job was working in an office, or collecting aluminum, we were to always be willing to do whatever it took to meet our obligations. During the summers before we went to summer school, we were required to go *"can collecting"* with her in the trash dumps of some of the most exclusive neighborhoods in Los Angeles. While this was embarrassing for a girl of fifteen, I learned that no job was beneath me.

I now work in an office and this lesson has served me well. While I don't rummage through the trash, there is no job that isn't my job. My attitude is *"I'll do whatever it takes to get the job done."* It is not about the pride that say's, *"I'm so great"*, it's about teamwork.

Everyone has to start at the beginning. Even the CEO's son has to start at the bottom. Not normally from a perspective of creating humility, but from the learning standpoint. The more you work within the ranks, the more you understand and identify with the people. You get to see first hand what they do day in and day out. You get to know them and empathize with them. These are the character building times in your life.

91 WORK TO FIND BALANCE IN YOUR LIFE

We spend so much of our time wrestling with the responsibilities of work, home, relationships, and sometimes we feel overwhelmed. When you are at that overwhelmed place, stop and look at what you really have to do—then do just that. Remember, while our lives are never without problems, we have a responsibility to ourselves as well.

Finding balance in your life is not always easy, because our lives are overrun with activities. A balanced life is never achieved. It is strived for every day. While we will never find a continued place of balance, when you are feeling out of sort, and overwhelmed; stop, revise and begin again.

92 LEARN TO NETWORK

In the world of business networking is essential to your success. Many don't know the true art of networking. Networking allows us to meet others that we can help and that can help us somewhere in our career. Part of the responsibility of networking is keeping in touch with that individual on a regular basis. Keep you name and what you do in front of them. Not in an obnoxious way, but just so they will remember who you are. Networking is about assisting your contacts in their endeavors, but also in seeking them when you need assistance. Again, we all need each other. We live in a social world. Virtually everything we do involves interaction with others.

There are many books on the topic. You've got to become a student of human nature. This is a social world and you are a social animal. If you are serious about a particular field, spend some time meeting those that would impact your field. Meet them, become familiar with them, do for them, and you will find others will do for you also. Careers are built on relationships—not on products or services.

93 FIND A MENTOR

We all need someone who has already accomplished what we want to accomplish to help us get there. These are the mentors in our life. When someone decides to *"mentor"* us, they have seen in us the desire that they had, and all the qualities necessary to reach the goal.

Look at your life. Do you have people in your life that are where you want to go? If so, demonstrate for them in very practical ways your commitment to reaching the goal, share with them your desire to have them mentor you, and watch them respond. When a person decides to invest the time in mentoring you, it says they see the success in you.

94 JOIN ORGANIZATIONS OF INTEREST

These days there are organizations on just about any and every career or interest you may have. Again, if you are serious about your chosen field, find an organization that supports what you want to do. Become a member, get active and develop relationships with the membership. Again, success is about relationship.

95 DON'T LET CLASS DIFFERENCE SEPARATE YOU

No one is any better than you and no one is any worse. We are all at different places. Some of us know more than others only because we have experienced more lessons. Share the wealth, but never think you're above others. The minute you begin to think you're above others is the moment you will be kicked down.

Begin to see people as people—not as their careers or their positions in life. Everyone looks to be accepted—to be included. As you show acceptance of all people—no matter what their station in life, you will find that people of all walks of life will uplift you.

96 MODEL PEOPLE YOU MOST ADMIRE

Like attracts like. Whatever we are or want to be like is what is attracted into our world. People seldom improve when they have no other model but themselves to copy after. While modeling is important, do not wish to be anything but what you are, and try to be that perfectly.

Who are the people you most admire? Look at what characteristics you find yourself attracted to, and use those characteristics to build your own foundation. As you purposely take them on, they will become habit in your life.

97 ASK FOR WHAT YOU WANT

We don't ask for what we want, we assume others will know or we don't feel worthy enough to deserve it. We don't ask because we fear rejection. I have learned that we may get what we ask for or we may not. Bottom line, you won't know until you ask.

Be bold, yet realistic. Don't be shy about admitting that you want some special things. The most you will ever get is the answer *"no"*, or what you ask for. There are only two responses to a question: yes or no. If its yes, you get what you want. If its no, you won't die, they won't kill you, you just have to ask someone else. No is not a fatal word.

98 PASS ALONG WISDOM AND KNOWLEDGE TO THE GENERATIONS

➜

"These commandments I give you today are to be upon your hearts. Impress them on your children. Talk about them when you sit at home and when you get up and when you walk along the road, when you lie down and when you get up. Tie them as symbols on your hands and bind them on your foreheads. Write them on the door frames of your houses and on your gates." —Deut 6:6 KJ

This is a powerful scripture about passing along wisdom and knowledge to your children and grandchildren. The lessons you have learned in your life can help guard your family from problems and harm, as well as breaking curses of past negative family behaviors and choices. This learning is not about sitting everyone down for a *"serious talk";* it is about the daily communicating with your children—communicating about the different situations they are faced with daily, and bringing your knowledge to them. While they may not always hear you, do your part. It is your responsibility.

99 WHAT IS—IS. WHAT ISN'T—ISN'T

This is a favorite phrase of my dad's. The understanding is to look at what really is, not at what we want it to be, or how it should be—but what really is, and learning to accept the reality of it.

What IS in your life that you haven't accepted yet? Is it the wealth you sister enjoys and you don't? Is it the job your brother got, when you feel he doesn't really deserve it? How about the privileges your little sister gets from your parents that you didn't get? If these are sore areas for you—*get over it!* What is—IS.

While you may have some valid concerns, you cannot change HOW someone is, or HOW someone decides to treat someone else. We must learn to focus on being our own very best self and not expend time and energy being jealous and envious of the successes and blessings of others. Think about it.

100 JUST DO IT

In its purest and simplest term this statement reminds us not to procrastinate. Don't make excuses. Too often we allow these very areas to keep us from achieving. When I began this project my excuses were, *"I'm too tired, too busy with housework, my job, my children, my grandchildren, etc."* I found reasons why I couldn't complete it. Not until I stopped the excuses, set a time frame, could I possibly finish this project. Express your goal in terms of specific events. Unlike dreams, which tend to gloss over important details, goals leave no room for confusion—they are detail oriented. Remember, goals need a vision. Get specific with tools like deadlines and vision boards. A vision board is simply a corkboard in which you display the goals verbally, display pictures of places you want to visit, things you want to have.

Nix the excuses. Just do it.

About the Author

Gina Johnson Smith has been a freelance writer for many years. Her articles have been published in local Southern California newspapers such as the Inland Valley News, the Walnut Times, the Pasadena Niche, and the Long Beach Times.

Through their organization, *Life of Faith Fellowship*, she and her husband Rube have been instrumental in teaching biblical wisdom and life skills to people of all walks of life.

Gina lives in Southern California with her husband, Rube, son, Chris, and granddaughter, Chanel.

Afterword

1 Cor 13:11-12

It is like this: When I was a child, I spoke and thought and reasoned as a child does. But when I became a man my thoughts grew far beyond those of my childhood and now I have put away the childish things.

In the same way, we can see and understand only a little about God now; as if we were peering at his reflection in a poor mirror; but someday we are going to see him in his completeness, face to face. Now all that I know is hazy and blurred, but then I will see everything clearly, just as clearly as God sees into my heart right now.

1 Corinthians 13:11-12 Living Bible Translation

These lessons are powerful in their urgency that we *"put away childish things".* Our life demands that we grow in the lessons put forth. Our decision is whether we will take the more excellent road and learn through our sages, or whether we will have to live out the pain of our lessons. It is our choice.

I hope this book has made you examine some areas in your life and has galvanized you to renew your mind and make the changes necessary for success.

The goal for us now is to clear up our hazy and blurred vision, and see as He sees.

God bless.

0-595-28290-3

www.ingramcontent.com/pod-product-compliance
Lightning Source LLC
Chambersburg PA
CBHW020243290526
45784CB00003B/1090